Out Of The Storm

A Message Of Hope, Trust & Faith!

Blessing E. Bassey

Out Of The Storm: A Message Of Hope, Trust & Faith!
Copyright © 2023 by Blessing E. Bassey

ISBN: 978-1639457649 (sc)
ISBN: 978-1639457656 (e)

All rights reserved. No part of this publication may be reproduced, distributed, or transmitted in any form or by any means, including photocopying, recording, or other electronic or mechanical methods, without the prior written permission of the publisher, except in the case brief quotations embodied in critical reviews and other noncommercial uses permitted by copyright law.

The views expressed in this book are solely those of the author and do not necessarily reflect the views of the publisher, and the publisher hereby disclaims any responsibility for them.

Writers' Branding
1-877-608-6550
www.writersbranding.com
media@writersbranding.com

Contents

Foreword v

Acknowledgement vii

Dedication ix

Chapter One

During The Storm 1

Chapter Two

Revelation and Restoration 19

Chapter Three

Distraction In The Time Of The Storm 29

Chapter Four

Perserving During The Storm 33

Chapter Five

The Power Of Forgiveness During The Storm 41

Chapter Six

Facing The Storm 51

Chapter Seven

Peace In The Tiime Of Storm 79

Chapter Eight
After The Storm, Don't Forget GOD
(The Blessing In The Storm)..85

Bibliography 106

FOREWORD

It is amazing how God sometimes reveals his love to us. The lord gave me the title of this book in the month of February, 2013; a couple of weeks after the hurricane sandy hit New York, also at the time I was coming out of a huge storm (a mysterious illness that almost took my life) including mental health, and eventually a brain surgery to remove a tumor from my brain which I miraculously made due God's divine intervention. I was walking on the road when I suddenly heard in my spirit: "Out of the storm!" So I picked a piece of paper and wrote it down and like a jolt, I heard again in my spirit, "You are out of the storm". At this instant, a chill came over me, and instantly I knew that the Lord is speaking again to me to write about it in a book. I can therefore say that this book is an inspiration from God.

ACKNOWLEDGEMENT

I acknowledge the Lord Almighty for the grace to start and complete this book.

I also acknowledge Ms Frances Ndika for helping to proof read, edit and make all necessary corrections. Thank you.

DEDICATION

This book is first dedicated to God almighty for bringing me out of the storm of humiliation, shame, poverty, sickness, marital turbulence, immigration turbulence and for giving me another opportunity to live again.

I also dedicate this book to God for giving me the inspiration and grace to start and complete this book. I am indeed very grateful to the Lord.

I also dedicate this book to all those that are currently experiencing storms in various areas of their lives. You will surely come out of it. Trust God and hold on. May the Lord strengthen you in Jesus' name, Amen.

CHAPTER ONE

DURING THE STORM

During the course of life, we are caught in a storm without any hope of how we are going to come out of it and we wonder where God is. We tend to question God for allowing us to go through a storm that almost ends our lives. We cry and say things to God we ought not to have said, we imagine things we ordinarily won't have dare to imagine but we always have to remember that Jesus Christ paid a huge price on the cross to bring us out of the storms of life.

During the storm we face lots of obstacles, hopelessness, fear, shame, stress, grief, misfortune, pain, poverty, sickness, joblessness, sickness, divorce and so many other negative issues of life. Life is a storm sometimes! Life can be tempestuous, tossing us with winds of misfortune and calamities. Jesus never at all-time promised us that life is going to be all rosy without pain and obstacles. In fact he said in John 16:33, that in this world we will face tribulation but we have to rely on the fact that he has overcome the problems of this world. *These things I have spoken unto you, that in me ye might have peace. In the world ye shall have tribulation: but be of good cheer; I have overcome the world.*

Faith is all about believing confidently that the journey ends well. And that's a cushion we can all sleep on. Sustaining faith is when God keeps you through the storm; Shadrach, Meshach and Abednego were fire proof. Don't complain about the storm for God is only bringing down the limitation that has been holding you back. The three Hebrew boys (Shadrach, Meshach and Abednego) were not known in the land as children of the highest God until they refused to eat the King's delicacies and also to bow down before his golden calf, and as a result were thrown into the fire. The fiery furnace which was meant to burn them to ashes became an air-conditioned room unto them, for the bible said they came out without the smell of smoke. God used the situation at hand to bring them out of the storm of slavery; they held on to their identity, serving and professing their God without fear. That storm broke down the wall of limitation upon their lives. Some years ago, when I totally surrendered to the Lord as my personal Lord and Savior, and master over my life; when I invited the Lord to have His way in my life, the lord spoke to me through the book of Isaiah. The revelation I got from the passage was that I should go back home to my father's house and reveal my new birth to my family, promising to gather me back to Himself. This is because as at this time, I was still hiding my identity in Christ Jesus from them because my family is Muslim. God provoked a situation that made me go home. Prior to this time, I had been married for about two years and still unable to join my husband who was in the United States. One day, I decided to fast and pray just for that purpose and this went on for three months with dry fast every weekend of those months. At the end of the three months the lord gave me a revelation about my father's house. He said that I should go tell my dad to take his hands off my marriage. So, I went home and told my dad what the Lord said and he was shocked but tried to argue his way out, but I told him I was acting as per the instruction from the Lord. Two days later he called me and begged for forgiveness, saying that he was told I was going to die if I remained married to my husband. By his action he thought he was protecting me because he was ignorant of the word of God and I told him I will not die because it is written that because Jesus lives I will live also. *John 14:19: After a little while the world will no longer see Me, but you will see Me; because I live, you will live also (King James Bible, Cambridge Ed.)*. After this incident, he started respecting the God that I worship, and also believed that this same God will deliver me from whatever they told him will happen to me. He practically left me in the hands of my God. Whenever we are experiencing storms in our lives, we should always look beyond it, seeing ourselves with the eyes of faith out of it because in the spiritual realm, we are really out of the storm. Your situation, appearance or personality might not look like it but be rest assured that the storm is working to bring out the glory of God in your life. Sometimes in life we go through some situation that makes us wish we were dead but because of our hope and faith in God we keep on holding on to God, trusting that He will show up for us at the nick of time. Did you know that the Apostle Paul was shipwrecked three times? We often times feel what Paul's shipmates felt during the storm that wrecked their ship; a shipwreck is something that no one wants to go through. **2 Corinthians 11:25 Thrice was I beaten with rods, once was I stoned, thrice I suffered shipwreck, a night and a day I have been in the deep.** Paul suffered so much storm that he wished he was dead but he however held on to God with the belief that the God that delivered him before is still able to deliver him, and will deliver him in future storms too. **2 Corinthians 1:10, He has rescued us from a terrible death, and he will continue to rescue us. Yes, he is the one on whom we have set our hope, and he will rescue us again, (International Standard Version);** a powerful declaration of faith in the midst of storm. Paul's story tells us that people can experience storms of life several times in life, nevertheless like Paul we should always be positive in life, believing that God can deliver us and will deliver us from all of them as they come. This is because He has done it before and is still able to do so again and again. In a time of storm, it is very important to remember people in the bible like Joseph, David, Daniel, Shadrach, Meshach and Abednego, Paul, Jesus Christ and so many others in the bible went through various type of storms and still had faith in God; they maintain their stand in the God they believe without wavering. We also should hold on to God like they did for by faith we will come out of the storm(s). When Paul was about to suffer a shipwreck with members of the crew, they noticed that the ship had been sitting in the waves of water heavy for three days and they thought that if they tossed some cargo overboard, they would be able to sail better and so they did but that did not help. So it is with us also; sometimes in life when we are mid-way into a storm, we tend to try different methods, ways and strategies to come out of it; we even try the help of men when actually our help in times like that is the hands of God alone. With Him by our side we can come out of any storm and there will be no trace of the aftermath like the case of Shadrach, Meshach and Abednego when they came out of the fire without any trace of fire burn or smoke. Even though Paul knew the outcome of the voyage would be disastrous and that no life would be lost, he still prayed, and even though he knew they would lose everything, he still trusted in God. It may be that while Paul was praying, he was asking God to prevent the loss of property and lives too, but it wasn't so in the end. However, God did answer his prayers because lives were preserved; it could have been worse if lives and property were lost in the storm. In life, we sometimes do not get the answers we are expecting to our prayers during difficult times, but this should not deter us from expressing our gratitude to God for when we do this, it shows that we are trusting and relying on the omnipotent and supreme God, concluding that He who knows best has done what is His plan and desires for our lives. We also honor Him when we do this. Is the ship of your life like that of Paul and wondering if you will ever get to the shore? Are you experiencing shipwreck in your career, marriage, ministry, relationship, health or life in general and asking; when will I get out of this? Jesus is our ship and unless you stay in Him as you go through the storms of life, you will be destroyed. In Matthew 14:22-23, when Peter stepped out of the boat to meet Jesus, he never thought about the storm and that Jesus was walking on the rough side of the sea, but when he took his eye off Jesus he began to sink but Jesus reached out His hand to him and helped him back into the boat, and the wave and storm ceased. Remember, Peter cried to Jesus to help him, how much have you cried to God for his help in times of storms of life? Most times, we are out of Jesus' reach, out of the boat of life and exposed to dangers in the world during the storm, yet the Lord keeps inviting us to come to Him. He said in Mathew 11:28-30 - *Come to me, all you who labor and are heavy laden, and I will give you rest. Take My yoke upon you and learn from Me, for I am gentle and lowly in heart, and you will find rest for your souls. For My yoke is easy and my burden is light."*

WHAT HAPPENS DURING THE STORM

FEAR AND PANIC - we fear and panic about the outcome of the storm and because of this we tend to look for easy ways out of the situation, thereby relying on our own wisdom and strength; we don't care about how those actions will affect others around us at that time. This is the major reason why suicide rate is so high nowadays; it's an easy way out. Alcohol, drugs, prescription pills etc are also other easy ways out. Rather than relying and depending on God with the hope that He will help us, we take the easy ways, which for the most part, are not God's way for us. Fear erodes our trust in God and we lose the grace to be bold (1 John 4:17-18).

There are several sources of fear and here are some of them:

DEVIL - the devil uses fear to impair our hearing in times of trials so that we do not hear from God concerning the issues that are threatening our lives at that time. No wonder the scriptures admonish us to not to fear several times in the bible. Fear can come in different forms - negative thoughts, depression, evil mentality, negative mindset, and negative confession/utterances. Until you can overcome your anxiety when God speaks, you will never hear the rest of what he has to say.

SIN – When we sin, the scriptures say the hedge of God is broken, we feel so vulnerable and we are exposed to the attacks of the enemies. By this we are ensnared by fear, which is one of the weapons of the enemy against our lives. Sin therefore brings about fear, and we are tormented by it. 1 John 4:18 says "There is no fear in love; but perfect love casteth out fear, because fear hath torment. He that feareth is not made perfect in love".

ENEMIES - the devil is a deceiver and he deceives us when he plants negative or evil seeds in our lives. When this happens, we begin to be afraid of everyone around us and begin to avoid them. Most times, we miss wonderful opportunities and people God brought our ways just because of fear of the unknown.

OURSELVES - we can be the source of fear in our lives when we like the other Israelite youths that Moses sent out with Joshua and Caleb to spy the land of Canaan. They devalued themselves when they came back with a negative report about themselves, but Caleb stilled them (Numbers

13). When we complain, worry, murmur, or allow anxiety to get hold of us, we invite the spirit of fear, which the Lord has not given to us (Timothy 1:7).

WE ARE TROUBLED – Our reaction to the storm has a great deal to do in defining if we are trouble or not. Oftentimes if not all time we are trouble. Instead of the disciples asking Jesus to lead them safely through the storm because of their faith in Him, they panicked and were troubled, they asked, "Teacher, don't you care if we drown?" Of course God cares, he is Emmanuel; God is with us. When we are troubled during the storm, the devil uses it as an opportunity to bring depression into our lives, and if we not snap out of it, it might lead to suicide.

WE PRAY LESS OR NOT AT ALL – It is so sad that in times of storm, most believers are so downcast and lose the power to pray; as a matter of fact, some do not even pray at all, hence the admonition from Paul that believers should always pray for one another. While some believers are unable to pray in times of storm, some others pray but with little zeal and thereby, unable to wait for the answers to their prayers. While Paul was going through persecution for his faith in the Lord Jesus Christ, the bible tells us that he prayed till he got answers from God. Even Jesus prayed so much throughout His earthly ministry which was laden with persecutions; even on the cross he was still praying. Are you in a storm right now? How well are you praying? Have you given up all hope for a solution or answer? I remember an incident some time ago which I will describe as the lie of the devil; it was in April 2013 after I recovered from a brain surgery that I had in July 2012. At this time, I had no job and was not able to pay my school fees, and as such could not register for the next term which is my last term. I felt so depressed for a long time that prayer became a stranger to me. It was so bad that the devil was telling me to write my will and leave all I have for my daughter. I kept hearing this voice inside of me until I suddenly jerked myself up and asked myself what kind of thought am I allowing to filter into my mind and why am I meditating on it? I got up and began worshiping God vigorously; I remembered how He saw me through the brain surgery, saved my life, and all His numerous blessings upon my life. I praised Him and thanked Him for His marvelous kindness to me and for His goodness, mercies, faithfulness and love for me and my household. I suddenly remembered that I am alive and that it is the work of the ALMIGHTY GOD alone and as soon as this realization set in, that depressive mood left me immediately. When I got home I took my laptop and started writing my third book which is this book. I AM ALREADY OUT OF THE STORM, but the devil wants to steal my peace and joy by making me feel downcast because of the situation at hand. I believe Shadrach, Meshach and Abednego prayed while they were in the burning furnace too and the Lord appeared in their midst as the fourth person there to comfort them; what a great God we have! Jesus shed His blood for us outside the gate to redeem us from the curse of the land. By this act, we have been delivered from every curse of the land which comes as storms now and then. Alleluia! **Isaiah 43: 2.When you go through deep waters, I will be with you. When you go through rivers of difficulty, you will not drown. When you walk through the fire of oppression, you will not be burned up; the flames will not consume you.**

God did not promise us a trouble free world but to be with us in each and every one of them. Many times, the storms of life bring about God's glory in our lives. In the story of Daniel and the lion's den, it was permitted by God in order to prove to the world that He is the Lion of the tribe of Judah, the all powerful and almighty, and bring glory to His name before the whole world. At the end of this event, the bible recorded that the king gave a new order and decree that made the God of Daniel the highest and greatest God in the land of Persia, and therefore to be feared and worshiped by all the people of the land. As long as you praise, worship, honor, serve God during your storm, and remain positive, walking in line with His word, your tests will become your testimonies, your triumphs. So stay in faith for He (God) is about to make your life a greater testimony. Bear in mind that God will use your storms to direct you to those in need; He is the one directing that storm in your life to stir your life to the direction He wants you to go. So, just as the aero plane soars high in order to avoid the storm while in the air and the eagle faces the storm and uses it to soar higher, we should quit trying to make things happen our way when going through storms but allow God to stir the boats of our lives. The wind (storm) will blow us into our destiny.

On your way out of the storm don't just look for your miracle but become a miracle. One test you have to pass is to be a blessing in the midst of your storm - ***Blessing Bassey***.

BENEFITS DURING THE STORM

Psalm 103 exhorts us not to forget God's benefit towards us; for though we face storms in life, God's grace is always available and sufficient for us hence we are able to endure the storm to the end if we faint not. Have you ever wondered how you survived the storm of joblessness, divorce or whatever storms you went through? Psalm 103 says if we have nothing to thank God for, we should thank Him for at least the gift of life; He is our sustainer and provider.

Psalm 108:1-8 -Bless the LORD, O my soul, and forget not all his benefits: Who forgiveth all thine iniquities; who healeth all thy diseases; Who redeemeth thy life from destruction; who crowneth thee with lovingkindness and tender mercies; Who satisfieth thy mouth with good things; so that thy youth is renewed like the eagle's. The LORD executes righteousness and justice for all who are oppressed. He made known His ways to Moses, His acts to the children of Israel. The LORD is merciful and gracious; slow to anger, and abounding in mercy. (New King James Version)

During the storm, there are so many benefits we have that we can't even see due to the physical or emotional turmoil we are experiencing. However, we should, like the psalmist here, try to remember all the benefits of God; He forgave our iniquities, healed our diseases, redeemed our soul from destruction, and has crowned us with His loving kindness. Oh, what an awesome God we serve! Can you imagine when King David thought he was actually going to die and God brought him back to life? The eagle's strength is renewed at its old age and it decides whether to renew its feathers and peak or to just wait and die. The eagle has the longest life-span of its species, but to get to this age, the eagle is faced with a difficult decision to take.

The Eagle is the most majestic bird in the sky, but something happens to all Eagles at least once in their lifetime, they molt. In the life of every Eagle, they will go through a molting process that can bring with it a great depression. This is a wilderness time that all eagles will face. Certain eagles live for about 30 years or more but then they begin to lose their feathers, their beak and claws begin to alter as well. The experts tell us brothers and sisters that during this time, the eagle will walk like a turkey and they have no strength at all to fly. The molting eagle finds himself in the valley, unable to fly, with its feathers falling out. They lose their ability to see, as well, their vision weakens during this time. Calcium builds up on their beaks and they can't hold their heads up. Now this is so traumatic, to the proud majestic birds that Eagles truly are. They lose their desire to eat, they only eat fresh meat and they have no strength to hunt. But then another phenomenon takes place. When the molting eagle gets in this last state, oftentimes they will begin to peck on each other, occasionally killing another molting eagle, as they gather together in one place. Now listen to this, at this time they will choose some area of a mountain range where the sun can shine directly on them, and they will lie on a rock and bathe in the sun. During this time some have observed other eagles coming and dropping food to the ones going through this "molting" stage. Yet it is never the younger eagles that are dropping the food, it is always the older eagles that have survived this experience and know what the "molting" eagle is going through. One writer, with knowledge of these things states...**(cite this please)**

"It is a most pathetic sight to see eagles molting in the valley, where they once would only soar over to look for fresh kill. However, if they don't renew, they will die " **(cite also)**

They grow weaker and weaker. Suddenly there comes a sound from the sky over the valley. Screaming loudly, another group of eagles fly overhead and drop fresh meat over the dying birds. The screaming is encouragement. That's what they reckon; the screaming is encouragement from other Eagles who have already gone through this. Some eat and recover but others roll over and die. Don't you think all of this speaks of something in our Christian lives as well? There is a time in the life of The Christian believer when it looks as though, and it seems as though. They've been stripped down to nothing. Let's look at some of the marks of this molting process the Eagle bird goes through; **The molting Process; (http://www.hopeinhull. com/Eagle%20Series.htm).**

The above analysis of the eagle and the storm as narrated above can be likened to the life of a Christian during the storm; he/she either chooses to dwell on or eat the word of God to renew us or to just give up on life and die. There is strength in the word of God; as a matter of fact that is the only source of strength for a child of God. People wonder why I always carry my bible at all times. The truth is that instead of reading books or materials that will not bless my spirit and soul, I choose to read my bible whether I'm on the train, bus or market. The bible is my only source of encouragement. As the older eagles bring food for the weaker ones to eat in order to survive, so does the Holy Spirit bring the word of God to our spirit and soul for our survival. We either choose to take it, meditate on it, pray on it and live or simply ignore it and die. As the weaker eagles are encouraged by the screaming of the stronger ones, so are we encouraged by the gently still voice of the Holy Spirit. Maybe you are currently facing a storm now as you are reading this book, I urge you to please turn it over to God and rest in His love and care for you. You will be renewed and live because God does not want you dead; you still have a lot to accomplish for your generation and the kingdom of Heaven. The essence of this book; OUT OF THE STORM is to exhort us that Jesus Christ is our substitute, so we don't have to go through storms alone and be expired by it. We are helped by the Lord to come out of them victoriously, renewed and blessed. Your sickness, poverty, shame, depression, hopelessness or whatever you are going through as a storm has already been dealt with on the cross of Christ. You are free but you have a choice to make. Jesus Christ our Lord tasted death for every man and we do not have to taste it again. When I was passing through the storm of infirmity in May 2012, I was only seeing death, and after I got out of unconsciousness several days after my brain surgery, I realized I could not walk; half of my body was numb but God delivered me so miraculously that till date, all I do is just to give thanks to God.

America, Canada and most of the developed countries of the world give benefits to their citizens, permanent residents who are not working, people who are unable to work, people who are on disability, etc. In Canada, women who stay at home to care for their children and or older parents are also entitled to benefits/welfare. These systems understand that women would love to work and make a living but these other responsibilities would not allow them to. So in order not to face poverty, they are given benefits in monetary terms to keep them going till the children are old enough to go to regular schools and they return to work. This is exactly what God does for us during the storm. He provides all that we need to survive till we come out of the storm. The blood of Jesus protects us till the end. When the devil's lie or accuses us during the storm, the blood of Jesus speaks against the devil by countering his accusation. There is power in the blood of Jesus to deliver us from the storms of life.

DECLARATION

I will fear not, for God is with me; I will not be dismayed, for He is my God. He will strengthen me; yea, He will help me; yea, He will uphold me with the right hand of His righteousness. **Isaiah 41:10** (Paraphrased by me)

I call forth every individual and resource assigned to assist me in the fulfillment of my kingdom assignment this season now. (Cindy Trimm).

CHAPTER TWO

REVELATION AND RESTORATION

The depth of the revelation we have about our situation will help to sustain us during the storm. Jesus was able to maintain his calm and focus on God His father on His way to the cross and on the cross because He had a revelation of the end from the beginning. He endured the suffering to the end; He was empowered and strengthened because of that revelation and so He was victorious at the end. Without revelation, we might never overcome and recover all. To overcome, we need to look up to Jesus: *Hebrew 12:2; Looking unto Jesus the author and finisher of our faith; who for the joy that was set before him endured the cross, despising the shame, and is set down at the right hand of the throne of God* Job 14:8-9 says that there is hope for a tree to grow after it has been cut down. It is only when the eyes of our understanding are enlightened will we understand and confess that all is well. In the time of storm, revelation gives us the strength to continue even amidst difficulties, pain, suffering, shame, poverty and so much tribulation.

In the year 2008, I was so financially constrained and had only $1.50 in my wallet. I wanted so much to go to church for bible study. In fact I desperately wanted to be in church that very day, for I felt in my spirit that God wanted me in church that day but was constrained by $2.50 for the bus fare to church. I stood in the middle of the living room and prayed for a miracle and all of a sudden, I had an inclination to check my winter jacket. Behold when I did, I found $1 and it made up the required bus fare and I quickly left the house for church. This experience remained with me till this day because before this incident, I had so much that I never imagined that there are people out there who cannot afford a $1 a day. Poverty is a storm and it is one of the storms I experienced in life and fought and prayed so hard that season of my life to overcome it. During this period of financial setback, God helped me with a job in a factory for $10 an hour, and also granted me favor before my neighbor who volunteered to watch my children while I go to work. However, this job did not last as just after a week at it, some of the workers including myself were asked to go because the work has slowed down. On the day we were asked to stop, I remembered standing at the center of the factory and asking God why me, and exclaimed; factory work again? God where are you? Where is that God that always provides for me even when I didn't ask Him; I just questioned God. In the midst of my pain and frustration, he answered me and said "it could have been worse than this "be grateful to me and start praising me". I was surprised, the devil actually had plans to frustrate me and hinder me from achieving my God given dreams through the spirit of frustration and poverty, but thanks be to God; the God of my fathers and ancestors, even the God of Abraham, Isaac, and Jacob, who is not a poor God. He delivered me out of the constraint and will deliver me again! So, I went to a corner in the same facility (the factory) and started praising God and all of a sudden the Supervisor came to me and said "what is your name? I told him, and then he said you can stay and continue working as long as you want. I was able to overcome here because I know my God as a provider, even my provider and had the revelation that He will yet provide for me here and He did; Alleluia! With Him there is no scarcity of the basic needs of life including money. I experienced God here as the restorer of good things. When we talk about revelations, we are talking about coming in the future or at the end of the world only but also something going to happen even in the present also. In addition, revelation is also viewed as now through the eyes of faith. In other words, when we get a revelation of the end of our storms, we are expected to begin to act it out in with faith because the bible tells us in the book of Hebrew 11 that "faith is the substance of things hoped for, the evidence of things not seen" (King James Version). We can therefore say we are already out of the storms of life by reason of Jesus Christ's finished work on the cross of Calvary; the bible says Jesus bore all our obstacles and misfortunes, He took all our sicknesses, sorrows, pains, poverty, shame, frustration, depression, hopelessness, stress or heartbroken. Are you facing any of these listed challenges or even more? I tell you, all you need is a revelation of God, as this revelation will make you view these challenges from a different perspective; the eyes of faith. I prophesy into your life that the season and hour of restoration is now; all that you have lost is being restored to you, and God is giving you back all the enemy stole from you. Amen and Amen! No matter what you have lost in life, the God that restored all Job lost to him is able to restore you back to your former position even in a double portion. The season of victory and restoration often comes with God's protection (1 Chronicles 4:9-10). He will protect all that concerns you including your salvation, peace and joy so that His name will be glorified as you continue to enjoy His blessings. God protects your joy so that you can enjoy your salvation (Isaiah 12:3). With the joy of the Lord, we are empowered to draw all we have lost to the enemy by faith in the finished work of Jesus Christ that brought about our redemption from the power of satan who has been the architect of your storms. He will restore, replenished and revitalized us back to where he wants us to be or what he wants us to be. Just trust him.

Oftentimes, when we are going through stuff in life, people around us might misunderstand and as such are not able to support or encourage you. Most times they don't even get it when you try to explain your pain, frustration and misfortune but thanks be to God that Jesus understands. Pastor Joyce Meyer once said in one of her telecasts that *"It is tough when you need encouragement and the people around you don't seem to get it"*. The only one we can truly rely on during the season of storms is our lord Jesus Christ. He is the closest friend in times of storm and also the only one who has the power to get us out of them; we need Him in order to experience restoration. It is a common thing for us to turn to our spouses, friends or relatives for help, which is quite natural. However, if we can go to Jesus first in faith with our problems, asking Him for a way out, He will surely show up. God said in the book *of Joel 2:25 - And I will restore to you the years that the locust hath eaten, the cankerworm, and the caterpillar, and the palmerworm, my great army which I sent among you.* God is in the business of restoring all we lost in life. After the hurricane sandy, lots of people were paid huge money by their various insurance companies to rebuild their houses, purchase new cars and replace lost properties. Just imagine God being your insurer, (remember the blood of Jesus is our greatest insurance in life); it ensures that everything taken from us can be replaced and even in greater ways than imagined. He is the only one that can replace live; His blood insures both the physical and the spiritual; the seen and the unseen; and the visible and the invisible; He does much more than all the insurance companies in the world can do. Some people lost their lives during the hurricane sandy and are gone forever and those with life insurance will have it paid to their family members but this money can never restore the dead back to life. Do you know that Jesus restored Lazarus, the Jarius daughter, and the widow woman on the way to bury her only son back to life? What an insurance we have in Him! As you are reading this book, ask yourself if you have a life policy with this man Jesus Christ. The major policy you need in life is the policy of eternal life (Salvation), and you can buy this policy without money, *Isaiah 55:1- 10: everyone that thirsteth, come ye to the waters, and he that hath no money; come ye, buy, and eat; yea, come, buy wine and milk without money and without price and Psalm 34:8 - O taste and see that the LORD is good: blessed is the man that trusteth in him(King James Version).*

In the realm of the physical, without money we cannot buy life insurance, and even when we have the money, we might still not be able to buy full coverage. Without the Lord we can do nothing; we need Him for everything including money for our sustenance. With the Lord, we have full coverage; physically and spiritually. May the Lord equip you with faith to believe that all you have lost in every area of your life – anointing for ministration, peace, joy, divine health, money, marriage, children, etc, shall be restored back to you. In the world, the insurance companies will only pay your claims to you after you have fulfilled their terms of service and this could be frustrating as these terms are in most cases difficult to fulfill but with God, His conditions for salvation (restoration) are carefully outlined in His word, the Holy Bible. It only behooves us to study them diligently to understand, and then do them. God requires us to come humbly to Him in total submission and repentance and He will honor His word of healing, peace, joy, restoration, promotion, etc; all these are in the salvation package. Do you trust Him enough for a revelation out of the storm of your life? Remember, by virtue of the blood of Jesus shed on the cross of Calvary you are already redeemed from the curse of the land, but you might not have this information unless you repent and turn to God. *Romans 8:2-3: For the law of the Spirit of life in Christ Jesus hath made me free from the law of sin and death. For what the law could not do, in that it was weak through the flesh, God sending his own Son in the likeness of sinful flesh, and for sin, condemned sin in the flesh:*

Revelation sees the restoration and faith takes it. Satan uses hopelessness to hold people down, so don't give way to the devil but draw joy from the well of salvation today.

God didn't take you out of Egypt to die in the wilderness but to make it to your promised land. Isn't it amazing how God takes care of us even when we are about to shipwreck? He tries to keep our eyes on Him and tells us that we will live through the storm. Even if the storm is of our own making, He still cares for and about us anyway. Because of His love and care for us, He always gives us the revelation we need in every situation to bring us out of the storm of life and grant us divine restoration.

RESTORATION OR BLESSING IN THE MIDST OF YOUR STORM

There are blessings at the end of every storm. Though the devil meant it for evil hence the fear, anxiety, worry, etc that they generate but God is able to and will turn them around for good. Left for the devil alone, his mission is to shake our foundation in God through fear, kill our faith, and get us off the track because he is a thief, a murderer and a destroyer. Thank God for His purpose for our lives which is for our good and not evil like satan's; so He will not allow the enemy of our souls to defeat us! He will calm us down, increase our faith, strengthen our foundation, and get us back on the right track! Remember the story of Job, how God allowed the devil to tempt him but the bible recorded that in all the storms of Job, he never sinned against God. God is also considering you now for a huge blessing after the storm like a job, so rejoice! What a joy to be considered by the creator! We might live our whole life or most of it in a community, city, or any place at that without being noticed by anyone, but it is not so with God. He takes note of each and every one of us daily. His ways are beyond our understanding, His wisdom is infinite and His compassion does not fail; it is unlimited. Surely we know that He will not allow any temptation to come upon us. Rejoice, knowing that God is counting on you to stand again on your faith in the midst of the storms! It is just humbling to know that God trusts in my capacity more than I do. The bigger the storm, the bigger the blessing!

Job is an example of the worst storms life can bring! Death of children, loss of property, loss of security, finances, family, friends! Destruction by fire, wipe out of everything meaningful and valuable! Loss of respect from family and friends, loss of power in community, loss of security, bank accounts, stocks, retirement, health care, home, car, clothes, money! Loss of health and strength! Loss of support for your spouse! Everything that supports and inspires one went in a single storm, but we all know the end result; God is awesome!

There is a blessing in knowing that the bigger the problem, the bigger the blessing God has laid up for you! If we make the right choices in the storm, we can reap the blessings of the storm! – culled from: ***Blessings in the midst of a Storm, By Samuel Stephens***

DECLARATION

A new cycle of victory, success, and prosperity will replace old cycles of failure, poverty, and death in my life.

I now have a new, refreshed, cutting-edge kingdom mentality.

I declare that there will be no substitutes, no holdups, no setbacks, and no delays.

CHAPTER THREE

DISTRACTION IN THE TIME OF STORM

Often in life, there are distractions at the time of breakthrough and elevation. The story in the book of Luke chapter 8 tells us that when Jesus was about to cross over to the other side of the sea with His disciples, there arose numerous smaller boats on the sea at the same time. Why was it so? The other side of the sea promises better things and the numerous boats on the sea at this time means slower progress in getting there. So also it is in life; we get distracted at the slightest chance of our elevation. It could come in the form of all manner of counsels from both friends and families, suggesting different ways of getting to our destination out of a good intention. However, it is very important for us to at this time listen to the Holy Spirit of God who is our guide and guard, hence the need to be spiritually sensitive. If we are not careful, we might just get confused on the way, and then come back to seek God's face again, and this we should have done from the beginning. At this stage in life, the gift of discernment is a very important gift we should covet.

Luke 8:22 - Now it came to pass on a certain day, that he went into a ship with his disciples: and he said unto them, Let us go over unto the other side of the lake. And they launched forth

It is not out of place for the bible to admonish us to be aware of the devices of the devil for he is a cunning being. He has a way of bringing distraction on our way just to cause us to derail and follow or take wrong steps that are contrarily to the will of God for our lives. In 2 kings 2:1, when Elijah was about to leave Elisha, the other sons of the prophets almost distracted him from the will and calling of God to and on his life; they made fun of him, telling him that his master was about to be taken from him but he (Elisha) remained focused to the end and got double portion of Elijah's anointing. The devil will do everything to take our focus off God when we are going through tribulations but we should always remember the promise of Jesus to be of good cheer for He has overcome for us. As I am writing this book, I am at the same time looking for a job, but having this deep impression to write this book; God told me some years ago about writing but I thought it was just my first book. I refused to be distracted with my unemployment status for I know that it shall come to pass too for everything that has a beginning will also have an end and I plunged into writing and surprisingly, this happens to be my third book! Storms never end because God did not promise us a crisis free world as believers. As we overcome one, another one shows up, even greater than the previous to challenge our faith further. Presently, I am battling with a career storm but I know my God will help and deliver me out of this too. Every one of us will receive a laugh, and a lift, and the motivation to go on to the next level in life, career, marriage, ministry, health and business in Jesus' mighty name. Amen!

Slow Living is the choice to live consciously with the goal of enhancing personal, community and environmental wellbeing. Slow Living recognizes the role that time plays in shaping the quality of our lives. By slowing down we make time to savor our experiences and to connect more fully with others. The process of slowing down involves simplifying our lives and minimizing distractions so that we have more time and more energy to focus on what is meaningful and fulfilling. By consciously choosing to do less, we contribute to reducing some of the negative social and environmental impacts of our actions. - *Slow Living from Wikipedia, the free encyclopedia.*

DECLARATION

I am a purpose-driven, kingdom-principled, success-oriented individual, and I refuse to be distracted by insignificant things and people.

CHAPTER FOUR

PERSERVING DURING THE STORM

As long as we are in the world we will face many storms. Here is the thing; Jesus did not promise us a problem free world; He in fact said that we will face many problems in life but that He will deliver us from all of them by His power therefore we should be of good cheer. It is important to note that storms are of different magnitude and length. For some people, their storm may just be for only a short period while for others, it may take a long period of time. All these are dependent on what God wants to bring out from our lives and also for His own glory too. God may just allow someone to go through a storm for a long period just for the person to mature spiritually and draw closer to Him. Y, the storm is then for good.

HOW DO WE PERSEVE DURING THE STORM?

Realize God's presence during the storms - Acts 27: 21-26 says no one on board ate for several days because of seasickness and fear. Paul and his companions realized the depth of the problem and knew death was staring them in the face. But when the storm worsens, Paul was at his calmest spirit since the storm. Acts 27:24 says *"For this very night an angel of the God to whom I belong and whom I serve stood before me, saying, 'Do not be afraid, Paul; you must stand before Caesar; and behold, God has granted you and all those who are sailing with you"*. Paul was at peace in his inner mind because he got an assurance from God that all will be well. God expects us to confess positively concerning our situation and to do this, we must have His word concerning that situation(s) and confess it for it is this confession of God's word in faith that brings about our liberation. Notice that Paul personalized God - "the God to whom I belong and whom I serve stood before". Just like Paul, we will do well by speaking the word of God to every mountain that is standing between us and our breakthrough for God expects this from us. Also, it is a declaration of our faith in the infinite wisdom and power of God. I will like to ask this question now: Whom do you belong to? If you belong to Jesus, you should be rest assured that His presence will never leave you. *1 Corinthians 5:3, Even* *though I am away from you physically, I am with you in spirit. I have already passed judgment on the man who did this, as though I were present with you. (International Standard Version 2012).* We might not see God physically but we should realize that he is always present with us in our life's journey.

Realize God's purposes and reasons behind the storms - Acts 27:9-20 - Our Lord allows storms to come our way for several reasons. For unbelievers, it could be God is seeking their attention for salvation and with believers it could be for several reasons that will bring glory to God as we can see from the lives of Job, Jonah, and the disciples of Jesus Christ in the New Testament. God used a storm to force Jonah to obey his instruction to go to Nineveh and preach His message to the people. This means we sometimes experience storms because of disobedience. It also means that God uses storms to direct our steps to the direction of our destiny. Jonah was trying to escape from the presence of God and boarded a ship to Tarsus but God intercepted him with a storm and when the captain of the ship and all who were in the ship realized Jonah was the cause of the storm, at his request, he was thrown out of it into the sea and the storm ceased. How many times have we run from the presence of God thinking we can have it our way but only to find ourselves in a greater storm, like Jonah? When he realized he could no longer run and hide from God he surrendered to Him and went to Nineveh to give the people God's message. At the end the people of Nineveh repented and turned away from their wickedness to God. Just as disobedience could bring storms our way, being outside the will of God for our lives could also bring storms our way. So what is the reason for the storm in your life now? Have you ever enquired from God why you are in this storm you are going through right now? Is there a storm in your career, marriage, ministry, relationship, business, etc now? Some of us are experiencing storms in our career because that is not what God wants for us or maybe we are in the wrong career. I was listening to Dr. Ben Carson in his book "Think Big". He said when he was in college he was going to be a psychiatrist because some of his friends were psychiatrists, but after a while he prayerfully thought of his decision and took an analysis of the kind of person he is and found that he is a very detailed person, careful and patient. All of a sudden it dawned on him that he will be better off operating brains and eventually settled for neurosurgeon. He is one of the best surgeons the world has today. Think, pray and mediate on the word of God for that career storm. Ask God questions about what he wants for you because his plans are better than yours for your life. Apostle Paul had a career as a Lawyer and was using it to persecute Christians till Jesus appeared to him and gave him a new career of going to preach the gospel to all nations both free and slave, rich and poor. Are you using that career to the glory of God or like Saul who later became Apostle Paul used his law career to persecute God's children? If you are, then you are heading into a storm. At times, God blesses us to bless his children. Some years ago the lord said to me "I am going to bless you but bear in mind that the money is for the work of the kingdom and not yours." After this incident, the lord has tried me so many times, asking me to give my last money to somebody or for something, I used to wonder how I obey even sometimes with tears in my eyes because in most cases that is the only money on me but he always restores. The main reason is because of where He is taking me to; He needed to trust me with His; to see how I will obey Him with them especially in times of storm. Recently, I left the book I was writing and went for a short training as a Nursing Assistant, and as I was about to start preparing for the state exams for the license that will enable me work in the state, I suddenly perceived in my spirit that it wasn't in the plan of God for me at that time, and the strength and inspiration to write came upon me there and then. So when I got home I picked my laptop and started writing.

In the case of Job, God permitted Satan to send a storm in his life by allowing the devil to destroy everything he has. In his grief, Job did not know that God had allowed this tragic storm in order to show Satan that he (Job) is God's servant and there was none like him on the earth, "a blameless and upright man, fearing God and turning away from evil" (Job 1). Have you ever realized that you may be God's instrument to demonstrate to put Satan to shame? We do not think in those terms but we need to. Sometimes the children of God face so many storms that the unbelievers mock them and ask: where is your God? Such a storm is for the glory of God.

Place your faith in the lord -1 Corinthian 10:13, There hath no temptation taken you but such as is common to man: but God is faithful, who will not suffer you to be tempted above that ye are able; but will with the temptation also make a way to escape, that ye may be able to bear it. John 14:27 - Peace I leave with you, my peace I give unto you: not as the world giveth, give I unto you. Let not your heart be troubled, neither let it be afraid., 2 Peter 1:3 Blessed be the God and Father of our Lord Jesus Christ, which according to his abundant mercy hath begotten us again unto a lively hope by the resurrection of Jesus Christ from the dead: 2 Chronicles 16:9 - For the eyes of the LORD run to and fro throughout the whole earth, to shew himself strong in the behalf of them whose heart is perfect toward him. There is every need for us to preserve during the storm by remaining in the word of God, Jesus overcame the storm with Satan by saying the word back to Satan "it is written…" we need to speak to our storm to be able to preserve through it.

The secret of remaining safe through the storms of life is to place your faith in the Lord, not place your confidence in the ship. He is the only one who can preserve us in our distresses. He is the only one who can calm the storms. Once we are brought to safety we are encouraged to give thanks to the Lord because he guided us to a desired haven. He himself is our haven – *James l. Goforth Jr. (Faith Baptist Church, Kaiserslauter, Germany)*.

Hope as your Anchor – sometimes it is your hope in God that serves as the anchor that holds. While the world rages, you simply hold on to your anchor. ***Lamentation 3:24 - The LORD is my portion, saith my soul; therefore will I hope in him****. Zephaniah 3:17 - **The LORD thy God in the midst of thee is mighty; he will save, he will rejoice over thee with joy; he will rest in his love, he will joy over thee with singing***. The greatest power we can use to anchor on hope is to believe the word and act on our belief, knowing fully well that we are only relying on the power behind the word.

DECLARATION

I will persist until I succeed.

I walk in dominion and authority. My life is characterized by liberty.

I wear the helmet of salvation to protect my mind from negative thoughts that would derail God's purposes and plans for me.

CHAPTER FIVE

THE POWER OF FORGIVENESS DURING THE STORM

The word of God 8 teaches us that forgiveness is a major key in keeping the devil away from us. Paul exhorts us to forgive so that we do not become victims of the devil's wicked plans. In addition, he used prayers to unlock the door of the future, thus forgetting the past and pressing on to the future. Paul knew that God was in complete control of the universe and of his life and did nothing without prayers; as a matter of fact, he does not stop praying until he gets answers from God. We should also imitate Paul in prayer by praying until we receive peace in whatever it is we are seeking God's face for. The word of God, the bible admonishes us to pray until our joy is full. In my walk with God, I have learned to pray over everything in life because I have come to understand the power of prayers and cannot have enough of it. I pray not only because I see the results by answered prayers but also because the kingdom of satan is disturbed and he and his cohorts are thrown into confusion, it brings me closer to God and I get to know Him better and enjoy intimate relationship with Him, and I also get to walk in victory, signs and wonders. Paul did not only prayed for himself but also interceded for other people included in this story, the very people who caused the shipwreck by not listening to him when he instructed them not to leave the ship based on the revelation he got from God. It is often not out of place for one to be filled hatred, anger and frustration during the storm towards those they think are responsible for their storms; this is because when we are going through diverse trials in life, if care is not taken we allow the devil to deceive us that a family member, friend, or other person(s) is/are the cause.

I have a brother-in-law (Apostle John A Bassey) who went through many storms some 4 years ago. During this period in his life, he was a subject of humiliation before his friends, some church members, some family members; he was humiliated and disgraced by these people and this made his case really heartbreaking. I wondered how I would have coped in his situation; would I have been able to handle it? I don't know. This same brother-in-law of mine has a wonderful job now even without work authorization or work permit in America, he is also married with a new baby boy. There is nothing God cannot do if we do not give up just like Apostle John. We will all agree that during this period he went through a lot of emotional, physical, and spiritual turmoil, but at the end, the living God showed up for him and he came out of the storm a new man with a new determination to serve God. The amazing part of this story is that he forgave all those who humiliated him especially in the public. Today, God has blessed him so much that those that ridiculed and laughed at him in the past are the same people celebrating and laughing with him and some also trying to become his friend again. God granted him favor with a full scholarship for his master's degree and presently teaching in a college where he earns so much pay. He has a home of his own, a car, and also two older girls that were born to him before and during the storm. In addition he has a ministry of his own where he is the pastor in charge with his wife; Lady Funmilayo Bassey. The blessing after the storm cannot be compared to the pain we go through in the storm. My brother-in-law was so humbled by God's grace, mercy and benevolence upon his life that he went and begged those who ridiculed him during his storm for forgiveness. Oh; what a heart! By this action of his, he humbled a lot of people, acknowledging the power upon his life. He is the author of the bestselling devotional, "Discover Your Life" and another life transforming book "I Saw Jesus So Can You". To me he is a wonder; God has made him a wonder for all to see. Didn't he say that no eyes have seen what he will do for us, nor any ear heard, nor has any heart perceived what he will do for those that love him?

1 Corinthians 2:9 - But as it is written, Eye hath not seen, nor ear heard, neither have entered into the heart of man, the things which God hath prepared for them that love him.

In the book of Genesis 30:1-20, we see how Jacob stole Esau's birthright and then his blessings. Esau wept so much that he asked his father if there was no blessing left at all for him, he thought his whole life was shattered.

Genesis 27:40 – "By your sword you shall live, and your brother you shall serve; but it shall come about when you become restless, that you will break his yoke from your neck."

He must have thought "will I ever make it in life"? What will become of me now that I have lost both my birthright and my father's blessing? Will I ever become somebody or be able to provide for my family? Or face my friends or colleagues? But Esau got a revelation that God has forgiven us our sins and mistakes both past, present and in the future. So, though he vowed he was going to kill Jacob after the death and burial of their father, Isaac, he had a change of heart and forgave Jacob even without Jacob knowing, because he (Jacob) was still far way in his uncle's village

(Laban). Esau forgave Jacob for stealing his birthright and God broke the yoke of bitterness towards Jacob off his neck, why? Because Isaac their father told Esau that the only way he can get out of the storm was for him (Esau) to break the yoke of Jacob off his neck and the father said to Esau that this will only happen "when you become restless". I want to believe that Esau became restless after he prayerfully made the decision to forgive his brother. God helped him by giving him the grace to forgive his brother from his heart. I also want to say here that the hurt of a relative such as a blood brother or a sister is the worst hurt anybody could bear or ever go through (if you doubt, ask Joseph). Because of what Jacob did, Esau faced the storm of uncertainty about his future – no birthright and no blessing. Oh! See how much God blessed him in Genesis 20:6, when Jacob returns home with his family and so much goods and property, he thought Esau will be in poverty as a result of what he (Jacob) did to him, but God who can change the tide of the storm and also calm the storm has changed Esau's story; he was already out of the storm; he refused gifts from Jacob, telling him without pride that he has more than enough. The power of forgiveness during the storm actually helps bring an end to it and releases us into our season of abundance. This is the reason why the devil does not want us to forgive; so that we will remain in darkness and continue in the storm, and if care is not taken, begin to murmur and complain against God, and also accuse Him of neglecting us in the storm of life. Hence the scripture says we should try as much as possible to live in peace with all men. We need to intentionally practice peace living. I once had a friend that used to tell us that whenever he feels somebody wants to offend him, he quickly runs away because it is difficult for him to forgive and forget. This is serious!

Hebrews 12:14- Follow peace with all men, and holiness, without which no man shall see the Lord.

Romans 12:18 - If it be possible, as much as lieth in you, live peaceably with all men.

Forgiveness during the storm is very crucial. When going through a storm or storms, you might be the one to go out and ask someone you might have offended to forgive you. This is exactly what Jacob did. Even though he was a successful and great man, he had no peace. This is because he stole his brother's (Esau) birthright and blessing. I believe God used his father-in-law to torment him to the extent that he thought within him, I need to go make peace with my brother Esau; *"If I can feel this bad over being deceived on a wife issue, how will my brother Esau must have felt that his destiny was at stake"?* The bible said, Esau embraced him which is a sign of acceptance. At the end Esau gave Jacob the staff of the blessing their father gave to him to deliver to Jacob, but

Jacob who was surprised by this gesture refused to accept it saying it rightly belongs to Esau but Esau refused, saying it is Jacob's by virtue of God's blessing upon him. Esau had the understanding that though he might be the first born, they both have different assignments and purposes on earth. It was after this incident that Jacob had peace and came out of the storm of fear and stopped being a fugitive.

Mark 11:24 is a blank check; "Therefore I say unto you, whatsoever things you desire, when ye pray, believe that ye receive them, and ye shall have them". Esau prayed and the yoke was broken from off his neck; Jacob prayed and was set free too from the enemy tormenting him from the inside because he was a sup-planter and trick star.

Forgiveness is key to our deliverance from the storms of life. Remember that Jacob told Esau that looking at his face was just like looking at the face of God. Unforgiveness can also close our heaven. In the case of Esau, it was unforgiveness towards and anger against his brother Jacob that kept him in the storm of lack of peace; he was waiting for a perfect time to strike at Jacob. Anger is listed as one of the deadly sins. *St. John Climacus states, "Anger is an indication of concealed hatred, of grievance nursed. Anger is the wish to harm someone who has provoked you. Irascibility is an untimely flaring up of the heart. Bitterness is a stirring of the soul's capacity for displeasure. Anger is...a disfigurement of the soul.*" (Rev. Fr. George C Mathew). It is the same for us too. We have to ask for forgiveness from God, accept it when He gives, and be reconciled back to Him and to others too if we must experience peace and calm in our inner selves. We have to be justified by faith. The main goal about forgiveness is where we go with it. Real forgiveness leads to reconciliation with Christ who states in the gospels that we must seek reconciliation with HIM and all mankind. There has to be sincere contrition of heart, and a real determination to make amends and to have a fundamental change of mind and heart so as not to offend God and man again. Otherwise, our spirituality has no truth and it is meaningless. Making amends often takes the form of restarting friendly communication; doing something nice that may be unexpected by the other; offering to help on a problem; telling a humorous story; or even resuming a previously halted activity. Real forgiveness moves past the roadblock and keeps moving forward.

It is important to note that forgiveness does not mean we necessarily forget, excuse, condone or demand some payback. If we can forget, it is a plus; forgiveness does not mean we have "'warm and fuzzy" feelings toward someone who may have offended us; it also does not mean we automatically trust anyone to act appropriately. No. Trust is a process and has to be earned in time by experience. And, if what was done affects the community, it may take time to be fully re-established in the community in the same status (occupation, style of life, etc.). But, if the person is repentant, we have to give the person the benefit of the doubt and be willing to trust. Our Lord reminds us in the Gospels about turning the other cheek and forgiving not just 7 times as the Law required (seven is a number representing completion), but 7 x 7 x 7 x 7 ... 70 times. That means you keep doing it in as much as God forgives us of our sins and shortcomings (Rev. Fr. George C Mathew). May the Holy Spirit grant us the gift of humility and real love to forgive and receive forgiveness.

DECLARATION

I have a fresh anointing that is uncontaminated and uncompromised.

By this anointing, every yoke is broken off my life and is destroyed; every burden is lifted. His yoke is easy and His burden is light.

CHAPTER SIX

FACING THE STORM

After a long day of teaching, Jesus Christ boarded a ship with His Apostles. They were going across the Sea of Galilee to teach the people on the other side. On the way, there arose a storm while Christ was asleep.

Mathew 8:23-24 says – "And when he was entered into a ship, his disciples followed him. And behold, there arose a great storm on the sea, so that the boat was being covered with the waves; but Jesus Himself was asleep".

The Apostles began to fear the storm as they were tossed by the winds. They awoke Jesus, crying, "Master, carest thou not that we perish?" (Mark 4:38). In facing the storm, we often forget about our God and look to man for a way out of the storm, but in reality man is limited. Like the disciples, we often times pray only when we are in danger and our lives and existence are threatened. It is so common for man to keep the Lord out of our ship and try to attend to the issues or problems of life on our own strength. The disciples here didn't bother with the Lord at the initial stage of the storm from my own understanding. I am pretty sure they must have thought they could handle the situation being professional fishermen but when reality set in, they cried to the Lord who has been there all along. It is so with us. When situations are minimal, we don't invite the Lord who is always by our side and with us but when they seem to be getting out of hand, we begin to panic, and then remember Jesus. We often try to figure issues out on our own but when our strength fails us, we then engage the Lord through prayers, seeking his face and help, which should have been done from the beginning. Facing the storm can be truly heartbreaking and threatening. Christ gently chastised the disciples for being fearful and not remembering that He is there and able to calm the turbulent sea. It is really unfortunate that many believers are really so fearful during storm or storms that they fail or forget God and so don't seek His face until things really go from bad to worse and worst. We need to face the storm with the assurance and faith that God is with us always like Queen Esther in the book of Esther 2, "if I perish, I perish". No matter how dark our conditions may seem in this world, no matter the condition of our homes, marriage, life, careers, business, ministry, families, etc. we can still experience the joy of God if we face the storm instead of running away from it. We need to confront our storm with courage, believing that God will see us through it to the end. In Isaiah 43:2, the word of God says - ***When thou passest through the waters, I will be with thee; and through the rivers, they shall not overflow thee: when thou walkest through the fire, thou shalt not be burned; neither shall the flame kindle upon thee. Deuteronomy 31:6, God said he will never leave nor forsake us.***

Sometimes God calms the storm but at times He uses the storm to calm His children. If Queen Esther had not faced the storm, all her people (the Jews) would have died or continued to suffer; living a life of slavery and misery. However, during and after the storm God gave them so much favor that affected their generations positively to date. Our faith in Him and obedience to His commandments will perfect God's will for our lives and brighten our hope. He will help us to overcome every despair and darkness in our trouble times. With the assurance of our victory through the blood Jesus shed on the cross of Calvary, we should be able to confront every giant of our lives with the confidence that Jesus has conquered the enemy for us. The time of storm is a time of life and death, and to triumph over it, we need God more than anything else in the world We must understand and believe that God is the only one that has the power to calm the elements of the earth and also to give us refuge from the storm. We can learn a lot from the life of the eagle when facing the storm.

Eagles never run from the storm when they are flying. Did you know that eagles can detect when a storm is approaching long before it breaks? When they detect storm ahead of them, they fly high above it and wait for the winds to come, and when it hits, they spread out their wings to the wind so that it will pick and lift them up above the storm. This should be the attitude of God's children during storms. We should be able to detect storms in the spirit before they come so that we can better prepare for them and in so doing, we will not be greatly hit by them. Pharaoh had a dream long before the storm of draught and famine hit the world which Joseph was able to interpret that led to his promotion from a prisoner to a prime minister in Egypt. The lord revealed to Pharaoh in a dream that there will be 7 years of famine after 7 years of bountiful harvests. He knew there is a servant of His there who will interpret the dream in order to bring glory to His name and also to promote his servant Joseph, and through him save His people; the Israelites. Just like the eagle, Egypt got this information and with the help of Joseph, whom God has ordained for this purpose, they were able to fly above the storm. Just as the eagle positions and prepares for the storm, as God's children, we also should be prepared for any storm God might allow for us. There is a popular idiom that says *"to be forewarned is to be forearmed"*, meaning Knowledge in advance enables one to be prepared. However, in preparing for the storm already foreseen, we need the help of God. This is why Proverbs 21:13 says *The horse is prepared against the day of battle: but safety is of the LORD*. I want to believe that if God had not sent Joseph ahead of time to Egypt, the nation would have been heavily hit by the storm of famine even though Pharaoh had a dream about it. The bible says that all Pharaoh's wise men and magicians could not interpret the dream to Pharaoh (Genesis 41.8). It was at this point that Pharaoh's butler remembered Joseph and he was brought in to the Pharaoh and when presented with the dream, he said *"I cannot do it," Joseph replied to Pharaoh, "but God will give Pharaoh the answer he desires."* (Genesis 41.1). When in a storm, we should always seek God's face for the way out and never rely on our own strength and wisdom; the time of storm is the time to seek the face of God not only for the way out which He knows but the purpose of the storm.

Pharaoh's Dreams as recorded in the book of Genesis chapter 41 (New International Version (NIV): When two full years had passed, Pharaoh had a dream: He was standing by the Nile, 2 when out of the river there came up seven cows, sleek and fat, and they grazed among the reeds. 3 After them, seven other cows, ugly and gaunt, came up out of the Nile and stood beside those on the riverbank. 4 And the cows that were ugly and gaunt ate up the seven sleek, fat cows. Then Pharaoh woke up.

5 He fell asleep again and had a second dream: Seven heads of grain, healthy and good, were growing on a single stalk. 6 After them, seven other heads of grain sprouted—thin and scorched by the east wind. 7 The thin heads of grain swallowed up the seven healthy, full heads. Then Pharaoh woke up; it had been a dream.

8 In the morning his mind was troubled, so he sent for all the magicians and wise men of Egypt. Pharaoh told them his dreams, but no one could interpret them for him.

9 Then the chief cupbearer said to Pharaoh, "Today I am reminded of my shortcomings. 10 Pharaoh was once angry with his servants, and he imprisoned me and the chief baker in the house of the captain of the guard. 11 Each of us had a dream the same night, and each dream had a meaning of its own. 12 Now a young Hebrew was there with us, a servant of the captain of the guard. We told him our dreams, and he interpreted them for us, giving each man the interpretation of his dream. 13 And things turned out exactly as he interpreted them to us: I was restored to my position, and the other man was impaled."

14 So Pharaoh sent for Joseph, and he was quickly brought from the dungeon. When he had shaved and changed his clothes, he came before Pharaoh.

15 Pharaoh said to Joseph, "I had a dream, and no one can interpret it. But I have heard it said of you that when you hear a dream you can interpret it."

16 "I cannot do it," Joseph replied to Pharaoh, "but God will give Pharaoh the answer he desires."

17 Then Pharaoh said to Joseph, "In my dream I was standing on the bank of the Nile, 18 when out of the river there came up seven cows, fat and sleek, and they grazed among the reeds. 19 After them, seven other cows came up—scrawny and very ugly and lean. I had never seen such ugly cows in all the land of Egypt. 20 The lean, ugly cows ate up the seven fat cows that came up first. 21 But even after they ate them, no one could tell that they had done so; they looked just as ugly as before. Then I woke up.

22 "In my dream I saw seven heads of grain, full and good, growing on a single stalk. 23 After them, seven other heads sprouted—withered and thin and scorched by the east wind. 24 The thin heads of grain swallowed up the seven good heads. I told this to the magicians, but none of them could explain it to me."

25 Then Joseph said to Pharaoh, "The dreams of Pharaoh are one and the same. God has revealed to Pharaoh what he is about to do. 26 The seven good cows are seven years, and

the seven good heads of grain are seven years; it is one and the same dream. 27 The seven lean, ugly cows that came up afterward are seven years, and so are the seven worthless heads of grain scorched by the east wind: They are seven years of famine.

28 "It is just as I said to Pharaoh: God has shown Pharaoh what he is about to do. 29 Seven years of great abundance are coming throughout the land of Egypt, 30 but seven years of famine will follow them. Then all the abundance in Egypt will be forgotten, and the famine will ravage the land. 31 The abundance in the land will not be remembered, because the famine that follows it will be so severe. 32 The reason the dream was given to Pharaoh in two forms is that the matter has been firmly decided by God, and God will do it soon.

33 "And now let Pharaoh look for a discerning and wise man and put him in charge of the land of Egypt. 34 Let Pharaoh appoint commissioners over the land to take a fifth of the harvest of Egypt during the seven years of abundance. 35 They should collect all the food of these good years that are coming and store up the grain under the authority of Pharaoh, to be kept in the cities for food. 36 This food should be held in reserve for the country, to be used during the seven years of famine that will come upon Egypt, so that the country may not be ruined by the famine."

37 The plan seemed good to Pharaoh and to all his officials. 38 So Pharaoh asked them, "Can we find anyone like this man, one in whom is the spirit of God[a]?"

39 Then Pharaoh said to Joseph, "Since God has made all this known to you, there is no one so discerning and wise as you. 40 You shall be in charge of my palace, and all my people are to submit to your orders. Only with respect to the throne will I be greater than you."

The above bible passage is inserted for us to easy grasp what we are saying about God preparing us to face the storm of life.

There need for to also remember that as Pharaoh was about to face 7 years of famine, on the other hand, it is a new season for Joseph, after 7 years of serving Pharaoh, he is about to be free and lunched into his destiny. See the verses below what Pharaoh said to Joseph.

Joseph in Charge of Egypt

41 So Pharaoh said to Joseph, "I hereby put you in charge of the whole land of Egypt." 42 Then Pharaoh took his signet ring from his finger and put it on Joseph's finger. He dressed him in robes of fine linen and put a gold chain around his neck. 43 He had him ride in a chariot as his

second-in-command,[b] and people shouted before him, "Make way[c]!" Thus he put him in charge of the whole land of Egypt.

44 Then Pharaoh said to Joseph, "I am Pharaoh, but without your word no one will lift hand or foot in all Egypt." 45 Pharaoh gave Joseph the name Zaphenath-Paneah and gave him Asenath daughter of Potiphera, priest of On,[d] to be his wife. And Joseph went throughout the land of Egypt.

46 Joseph was thirty years old when he entered the service of Pharaoh King of Egypt. And Joseph went out from Pharaoh's presence and traveled throughout Egypt. 47 During the seven years of abundance the land produced plentifully. 48 Joseph collected all the food produced in those seven years of abundance in Egypt and stored it in the cities. In each city he put the food grown in the fields surrounding it. 49 Joseph stored up huge quantities of grain, like the sand of the sea; it was so much that he stopped keeping records because it was beyond measure.

In early 2007, while I was still in the United Kingdom, I had a revelation from the book of Judges when the Amalekites were destroying the harvest of the children of Israel; I had this revelation three times, and had to go discuss it with my local church pastor. I told him about the dream and emphasized that when God reveals something to me three times, it will surely come to pass unless it is counteracted with serious fasting and prayers or a higher anointing. I understood from the dream that hardship and suffering awaits me in Canada, as this dream came when I was preparing to relocate to Canada. So I told him I don't want to go to Canada because of this but he did not believe me and using the scripture, he counseled me that it supports husband and wife living together so as not to give room to Satan. He prayed with me and I relocated to Canada, and when I got there, I told my husband the dream I had while in London but he didn't take the dream seriously and therefore did hearken to my warning; I was taken for granted, so I forgot about it. After some months, my husband got some money and invested it in a business in Canada but that business was seriously attacked spiritually that even those who were not Christian knew something was wrong; we lost both capital and profit, and all the years I spent in Canada were years of financial poverty. This is the kind of poverty that you seem not to have any choice, but God helped us. The money my husband borrowed is still being settled till date. I learned a lesson from this experience and pray that God will never allow me to mess up like this again. The eagles don't wait for anyone to cooperate with them; they soar through the storm alone because they already have the information of the wind and are prepared for it. This financial storm brought forth three children by God's infinite mercies, and we were able to comfortably take care of them. Also, God gave me perfect health that I was able to do most things new nursing mothers are not able to do just a few weeks after birth, such as resuming church activities immediately after my baby's naming ceremony. To God be the glory, the storm is over in our lives, though the devil sometimes tries to make it look like we are still in it but we are way far ahead in Jesus name. We were able to face this storm with the faith in the God never leaves or forsakes His own; who is faithful to His promises to be with us through fire and water. We had faith and trust in him but we also prayed and were fully engaged in the work of God. Remember that while Joseph was still in the prison, he was always cheering the other prisoners up and it was in the cause of this that he met the Pharaoh's Butler who later recommended him to Pharaoh to interpret his dream. Some Christians, when in a storm, get angry, frustrated and leave the church. It ought not to be this way. We should like Joseph continue to do the good works that will please God knowing the covenant keeping God will keep His promises concerning our lives as we do our part to obey Him. May the Lord grant you the strength you need to remain in his service in Jesus' name. Amen.

Isn't it remarkable that the eagle soars above while the storm is raging below? The eagle does not cower down during the storm but uses it to lift itself higher. It rises on the winds that bring the storm and soars higher so above it. What an extraordinary way to deal with adversity! – Culled from, *To Soar Like Eagles by Randy Vild.*

Just like Esther, Ruth and Joseph, who soared high above the storm raging against their lives and destiny, we should also learn from their experiences and do same. Joseph soared high above the storm by maintaining his joy even in the prison. Ruth soared through the storm by maintaining her faith, trust and confidence in the God of her mother in law's (Naomi) God; the God of Israel. Esther soared high above the storm by waiting on the Lord God of the Jews in fasting and prayer and, instead of a death sentence she was granted divine favor before the King. Like the eagle you too can soar high above the storm as it comes. But on what do you hold onto as you soar? Joseph held on to the joy of God. Isaiah 12:3 says you will draw water with joy out of the well of salvation. In the well of salvation there is hope, healing, prosperity, success, joy, victory, blessings, promotion, grace, favour, deliverance etc. What are you holding on to in Christ Jesus? It is significant to understand that what you hold onto during the storm is very important. I believe Esther must have mastered the art of fasting and prayer while still living with Mordecai and had come to know that it makes way for people before God, hence when she came to a dire situation in the palace, she requested that all her people fast with her for favor before the king. Now the fasting was to seek God's face for the storm and God showed up for her at the end. When David was to confront Goliath he rejected the garment of war given to him by King Saul for according to him, it was new to him and he does not have a mastery over it. He therefore put on the garment of confidence in the God of his fathers which he has tested and proven to be effective. With this garment, he killed the bear, lion and other dangerous animals that threatened him and his cattle in the bush. So he went to battle with Goliath with just a sling and God gave him victory. I have also learned to turn to the bible whenever I am going through any kind of storm in life and pray the promises of God to my life. I learned early in my Christian life, while still in college, to wake up early to pray and study God's word before studying for my school books and I never failed any course from beginning to the end of my undergraduate program. My love for the study of God's word brought out my gift in writing. The Holy Spirit used to enlighten my understanding through the scripture in solving problems in English language and grammar. My friends in church often make fun of me whenever I use the scripture to analyze English Language and grammar. This made me believe that all discipline has its root in the bible. Prior to this time, I had problems with English language and grammar, and actually struggled to pass it in high school, and for real spent several years at home after high school studying and retaking it in my senior secondary certificate known as GED in the US. I needed to pass it before securing a place in college, but today, God used the bible to give me a fluent understanding of the language; the same person who struggled with English language and grammar is the one writing books and messages today. With God's help, I overcame the storm. What are we saying here? There must be something you do with ease when it comes to God and this particular thing has helped you to face so many storms in the past. Hold on to that thing, God can and will still use it to help you through any storm in life. There is a popular Pastor in Nigeria who during his youth, was very deep into drug that he almost went mad. His parents sent him overseas to study and he ended up with friends who were addicted to drugs and became an addict too. His mother who fortunately happens to be a prayer warrior prayed till the heaven over her son opened and today that same son is a Pastor and his ministry includes bringing souls bound by satan to drugs to Christ. In the encounter with Moses in Exodus 4, When he complained to God that he is not fit to carry out the Lord's assignment of delivering His (God) people out of the hands of Pharaoh, God pointed to him the rod in his hand, and showed him how it can be put to use in this assignment when with God's instructions, the rod turned snakes and swallowed up Pharaoh's magicians' snakes - Exodus 4:1-5, Moses objected, "They won't trust me. They won't listen to a word I say. They're going to say, 'God? Appear to him? Hardly!'"

2 So God said, "What's that in your hand? "A staff."

3 "Throw it on the ground." He threw it. It became a snake; Moses jumped back—fast!

4-5 God said to Moses, "Reach out and grab it by the tail." He reached out and grabbed it—and he was holding his staff again. "That's so they will trust that God appeared to you, the God of their fathers, the God of Abraham, the God of Isaac, and the God of Jacob."

Like Moses in the above conversation with God, some of us don't know the power we have when we face the storm, till we turn to God to help us to see that the strategy to overcome the storm is always with us. Very few people already have a revelation or understanding of how God always shows up for them using what is with them to take them through the storm. Some Christian sisters are facing the storm of how to get a good husband and age is no longer in their favour, they weep and complain all the time, while some decides to use the time of waiting for the glory of God by putting their entire live into the work of God's kingdom, and when they eventually gets married, things, move so fast for them that you won't but wonder what kind of God they serve. I know of a fellow sister in the church that was very advance in age and also a professional in career, she very fervent in the things of the kingdom, but a day came she was so depressed that she almost committed suicide, the had to call her and prayed for her, within six months after this incident, a brother from the church went to see the pastor that he was interested in the sister, they eventually got married and now expecting their first child. God remembered her simply because of her interest in the things of the kingdom. Have you been working for the Kingdom and still facing storms? God will have mercy and very soon that storm will be over. *Psalm 102: 13-14 Thou shalt arise, and have mercy upon Zion: for the time to favour her, yea, the set time, is come. For thy servants take pleasure in her stones, and favour the dust thereof,*

A LESSON FROM THE EAGLE DURING A STORM

During a storm, the eagle flies above it in order to overcome it. He does this in a very interesting way; He uses the strength of the storm to rise above it. That is one of the things God wants us to do. We can use adversity for gain. When God allows trials in our lives, He wants us to learn from the experience and grow into a more matured man/woman. James 1:2-3 says: "James, a servant of God and of the Lord Jesus Christ, to the twelve tribes which are scattered abroad, greeting. Knowing this, that the trying of your faith worketh patience".

The way and manner the eagle rises above the storm using its strength is a great lesson for us Christians to learn from. When the storms of life come upon us, we, too, can use the strength of the storms to rise above them. We can do this by setting our minds and our hearts toward God. The storms do not have to overcome us any more than they overcome the eagle. We can lean on God's power, allowing it to lift us above them. The storms (or trials) of life can actually help to increase our faith in God. This is because they help us to develop a resistance in us that will be a part of our lives forever. Notice what Paul wrote to the congregation at Corinth. *"For our light affliction, which is but for a moment, is working for us a far more exceeding and eternal weight of glory" (2 Corinthians 4:17).* How true this is for Joseph who had to endure humiliation, slavery, false accusation, abandonment and imprisonment, and ended up with a royal and prestigious position as the Prime Minister of Egypt. All the storm did for him was to endow him with wisdom and strength, which he never had at the beginning to handle the difficulties that came his way, and occupy his destiny.

Some years back while still in my home country Nigeria, I was so heavily burdened and pressed down with so many trials and troubles that I was forced to go and see one of the senior pastors in the Redeemed Christian Church of God; Pastor J.T. Kalejaiye and when I came to him, before I could say a word to him, he told me I am passing through storms in my life because of my destiny, and the reason for them is to prepare and propel me to my destiny. He told me he wasn't what he was at the time I saw him on that day and if I had known him before that day, I wouldn't believe what I was seeing. He then told me that as God dealt with his storms, he will deal with mine also.

If I hadn't gone through those storms then, I probably would not have been able to overcome the subsequent storms that followed later in my mind, and with each victory comes another one. God is faithful and my ability to stand firm in all of them comes from Him alone. Sometimes we should "escape" trials – "There hath no temptation taken you but such as is common to man: but God is faithful, who will not suffer you to be tempted above that ye are able; but will with the temptation also make a way to escape, that ye may be able to bear it" (1 Corinthians 10:13). Sometimes we should "flee" "But when they persecute you in this city, flee ye into another: for verily I say unto you, Ye shall not have gone over the cities of Israel, till the Son of man be come" (Matthew 10:23). When the Philistines were contending with Isaac over his wells by closing them up after he dug them, he kept fleeing from them until they became tired. However, there are times we should confront trials (2 Thessalonians 1:4; 2 Timothy 4:5; Hebrews 12:7).

We must face the things that challenge us and grow in virtue because of the challenge bearing in mind that Jesus already paid the price of whatever storm we are encountering or going to encounter in life.

God is looking for overcomers. And He has a wonderful promise for them. "To him who overcomes I will grant to sit with Me on My throne, as I also overcame and sat down with My Father on His throne" (Revelation 3:21).

7 PRINCIPLES OF AN EAGLE

– By Dr. Myles Monroe

PRINCIPLE 1

Eagles fly with Eagles. Eagles fly alone at high altitude and not with sparrows or other small birds. No other bird can get to the height of the eagle. Stay away from sparrows and ravens.

This principle goes with *Proverb 27:17 - Iron sharpeneth iron; so a man sharpeneth the countenance of his friend*. In facing the storm, not every friend or relative will be helpful, so you should be vigilant in choosing who you want to fly with at every storm of life. It is not everyone in your church that will be useful to you during a storm. As a matter of fact you may need to practically run away from some people, not because they are bad but because they are not useful to you at this stage. You need somebody to strengthen and encourage you. This what the eagle does when facing the storm; they look for eagles like themselves to soar with or soar alone with their trust in God who can see them through it. There are some storms that is just between you and your God, if God doesn't help you, nobody can.

PRINCIPLE 2

Eagles have strong vision. Eagles have the ability to focus on something up to five kilometers away. When an eagle sites his prey, he narrows his focus on it and set out to get it. No matter the obstacles, the eagle will not move his focus from the prey until he grabs it.

Have a vision and remain focused no matter what the obstacle may be and you will succeed. Jesus Christ had a vision of getting to the cross and despite all the devil tried to do to him (shame, humiliation, pain, false accusation, death), he never gave up, but remained focused to the end.

Being focused on what is ahead of us helps us to remain strong and positive in the midst of adversity or storm. It gives us courage from within us that propels us towards our goal just like the eagle.

PRINCIPLE 3

Eagles do not eat dead things. Eagles feed only on fresh prey, they only eat fresh animals unlike the vultures that eat dead animals.

Be careful with what you feed your eyes and ears with during the storm, especially in movies and on TV, and also advise from people. Steer clear of outdated and old information. Always do your research well.

I will say from experience that it is what you feed your eyes and ears on that will eventually take over your spirit man. This principle says eagles do not eat dead things, what are dead things to us? These are things that are detrimental to our destiny and life in general. Things that will distract our attention and hinder us from our destinies. Sometimes, if not rightly focused, we might not be able to overcome the storm or come out of it very hurt.

PRINCIPLE 4

Eagles love the storm. When clouds gather, the eagles get excited. The eagle uses the storm's wind to lift it higher. Once it finds the wind of the storm, it uses the raging storm to lift itself above the clouds. This gives the eagle an opportunity to glide and rest its wings. In the meantime, all the other birds hide in the leaves and branches of the trees until the storm is over, and in most cases, depending on the severity of the storm, they hardly make it alive.

We can use the storms of life to rise to greater heights. Achievers relish challenges and use them profitably.

PRINCIPLE 5

The Eagle tests before it trusts. When a female eagle meets a male and they want to mate, she flies down to earth with the male pursuing her and she picks a twig, and then flies back into the air with the male still pursuing her.

Once she has reached a height high enough for her, she lets the twig fall to the ground and watches it as it falls. The male chases after the twig. The faster it falls, the faster he chases it. He has to catch it before it falls to the ground. He then brings it back to the female eagle, who will grab it and flies to a much higher altitude and then drops it again for the male to chase. This goes on for hours, with the height increasing until the female eagle is assured that the male eagle has mastered the art of catching the twig which shows commitment. Then and only then will she allow him to mate with her.

Whether in private life or in business, one should test commitment of people intended for partnership. This should also be applied during a storm. Testing for commitment will go a long way in saving us when facing the storm or avoiding it altogether. The female eagle might want to know how well the male eagle will react when there is storm; whether he will be reliable or not.

PRINCIPLE 6

When ready to lay eggs, the female and male eagle identify a place very high on a cliff where no predators can reach. The male flies to earth and picks thorns and lays them on the crevice of the cliff, then flies to earth again to collect twigs which he lays in the intended nest. He flies back to earth and picks thorns, laying them on top of the twigs. He flies back to earth and picks soft grass to cover the thorns. When this first layering is complete the male eagle runs back to earth and picks more thorns, lays them on the nest; runs back to get grass and put on top of the thorns, then plucks his feathers to complete the nest. The thorns on the outside of the nest protect it from possible intruders. Both male and female eagles participate in raising the eagle family. She lays the eggs and protects them; he builds the nest and hunts. During the time of training the young ones to fly, the mother eagle throws the eaglets out of the nest. Because they are scared, they jump into the nest again.

Next, she throws them out and then takes off the soft layers of the nest, leaving the thorns bare. When the scared eaglets again jump into the nest, they are pricked by thorns. Shrieking and bleeding they jump out again this time wondering why the mother and father who love them so much are torturing them. Next, mother eagle pushes them off the cliff into the air. As they shriek in fear, father eagle flies out and catches them up on his back before they fall and brings them back to the cliff. This goes on for sometime until they start flapping their wings. They get excited at this newfound knowledge that they can fly.

The preparation of the nest teaches us to prepare for changes; the preparation for the family teaches us that active participation of both partners leads to success; this pricking by the thorns tells us that sometimes being too comfortable where we are may hinder our learning and progress in life. The thorns of life teaches us to get out of our comfort zone and grow in life. We may not know it but the seemingly comfortable and safe haven may not really be what we think it is. So we sure need thorns to get out of that zone and soar to the utmost top.

The people who love us do not let us languish in sloth but push us hard to grow and prosper. Even in their seemingly bad actions they have good intentions for us.

PRINCIPLE 7

When an Eagle grows old, his feathers become weak and cannot take him as fast as he should. When he feels weak and about to die, he retires to a place far away in the rocks. While there, he plucks out every feather on his body until he is completely bare. He stays in this hiding place until he has grown new feathers, then he can come out.

We occasionally need to shed off old habits and items that burden us without adding to our lives. Old habits might not help us in facing the storm when it comes. And if our old habits don't had value to our lives than we do not need to hold on to them but shed them off, otherwise they will be unnecessary burdens that will add to our struggles.

Sometimes in life we face storms that require us to humble ourselves or lower our standard. It also mean increasing our standard – Blessing Bassey.

DECLARATION

Father, I pray:

Close the gates of death and seal up the doors of affliction and torment.

Assign angels as my supernatural escorts and supernatural security. Let them marshal the boundaries and borders of my spheres of influence. Let them dismantle and destroy satanic strongholds and dispossess satanic squatters.

Cause the east winds of judgment to blow into the enemy's camp. Stop the diabolical cyclones and demonic winds designed to bring shipwreck and disaster into my life.

Grant me divine kingdom asylum and diplomatic immunity from evil that seeks to imprison and entrap me.

Synchronize my life with Your perfect will, agenda, and calendar.

Amen.

CHAPTER SEVEN

PEACE IN THE TIME OF STORM

Matt 4:16 – The people which sat in darkness saw great light, and to them which sat in the region and shadow of death light is spring up. What this verse is saying is that as long as you remain in Christ you will have peace because the light of God will always shine on you and around you, in short everything you do will receive light, and where there is light, darkness cannot dwell and where darkness cannot dwell there is peace. In Matt 8:23-24, the bible says in the midst of the storm, Jesus was asleep, that is how believer are supposed to live in the season of storm; having the full assurance that Jesus has calmed every storm in our lives. He said to his disciples "be of good cheer for I have overcome the world", that is, be calm in the hour or season of storm, have trust in his word that all the storm we are going to face in life has been taken care of on the cross and based on his word. The blood of Jesus has already calm our storm both today and in the future.

Peace may not always come as it did that long-ago day on Galilee—the storms and winds may not be replaced by perfect calm. But, when we hasten to call on the Master and allow Him to bear our burdens, our peace may come in small reminders of His love and care, giving us strength to get through the storm *—Culled from "Facing the Storm of Life" by Whitney Hinckley.*

Do you know Christ not only calms the physical seas, but also calms the seas within our minds and souls if we allow him? Some years ago, it was three years into my marriage, I experienced a severe hatred from my husband's family that made me start wondering what was wrong, because they don't know me before, but were bent on destroying my marriage. Then I remembered the lord led me into this marriage, so I went to God in fasting and prayers. One night during this fasting and prayer, I slept and saw myself in a very long corridor of a house with several old women but one particular old woman refused to allow me to pass through the corridor to get out of the house. She blocked my way with her hands spread wide on the door with a stern and evil look on her face, and I, refusing to back off, rebuked her in the blood of Jesus and I pushed her out of my way. Immediately a wind came and violently threw her out of my way and I ran out of the corridor into the open space. When I saw my dad a couple of weeks later, I told him what I saw by describing the woman to him. He was shocked and said that a woman laid a curse on his father's house that no marriage in that family will ever have peace. According to him, the story has it that the woman was married in his father's house and had one son, and that his father's house used to serve idols that required a sacrifice of human blood. This woman's only son's blood was donated to the idol even against her wish; all her appeal not to sacrifice her only son fell on deaf ears, so she laid a curse on that family that no marriage in the family will ever have peace. My father's female siblings never had a peaceful marriage; they always came back home to their father's house and the male children too had rough marriages; even their children could not stay in their matrimonial homes too as they had no peace. This curse was laid many generations ago. My father was the only one that kept his family till the end of his life and had all his children from one woman. When I got married I never had peace, there was so much confusion, hatred and wickedness. I could not please my husband's family as much as I tried, as everything I did or said seems to be the wrong thing. I was so accustomed to peace that it was easy for me to notice something was wrong then. I needed the peace of God so I cried to God for days, and one morning the lord said to me "you are a chosen generation", "a new generation", that my generation is not cursed. The lord confirmed this two days later on the monthly Holy Ghost service of the Redeemed

Christian Church of God through the general overseer Pastor E.A. Adeboye. During the Holy Ghost service, I stood facing him, and in my spirit I was prayerfully waiting for him to say something and towards the end of the service, at about 4 a.m., he said there is a woman here, God said "I should tell you that the curse upon your family has been broken". I shouted hallelujah and started praising God. After this incident, God restored back my peace, and this is the confidence that I have that the curse indeed is broken. However, the devil is not giving up but trying to reactivate what God has destroyed and nullified. Some people are living their lives without the peace of God just because the devil has stolen it. In everywhere they turn, there is no peace and whatever they do, they never experience the peace of God. Whatever it is that is stealing the peace in your career, marriage, health, business or children's lives, in this year of the Lord, the God that showed up for me and delivered me will show up for you, your family and children too. When the disciples were afraid of the storm, the bible said Jesus was fast asleep, I tell you, from now on, when storm comes to steal your peace, you won't even notice it like Jesus, you will be fast asleep, you will wake up, rebuke the storm and continue your life. A very popular General Overseer in Nigeria, Pastor Oyedepo (Winners chapel) use to say people always ask him why he is always happy and that its like he has no problem, he said he always reply that "maybe the problem came and he didn't notice it", this will be your testimony from now on. God sees your future, whatever is going to steal your peace during any storm has already been taken care of. I pray that you will receive this revelation and grace will be given you to maintain your peace.

It's hard to remember there is someone who can bring peace when we are being tossed so hard that we feel like we can barely hang on. Sometimes in life we just try to outlast the storm, forgetting to call on the One who can calm it. Culled from *"Facing the Storm of Life" by Whitney Hinckley.*

DECLARATION

Father, in the name of Jesus, I decree and declare:

I speak peace into my life, relationship, ministry, workplace and business.

I have the peace of Christ Jesus which passeth all understanding.

The Lord will keep me in perfect peace because my mind is stayed on him and I trust in him.

The LORD gives strength to his people; the LORD blesses his people with peace. – Psalms 29:11

Consider the blameless, observe the upright; there is a future for the man of peace - Psalm 37:37

I will listen to what God the LORD will say; he promises peace to his people, his saints-- but let them not return to folly. Psalm 85:8

Great peace have they who love your law, and nothing can make them stumble. Psalm 119:165

CHAPTER EIGHT

AFTER THE STORM, DON'T FORGET GOD (THE BLESSING IN THE STORM)

Don't forget what it took God to get you to where you are; pass God's goodness to the next generation – Joel Osteen.

It is very easy for us to forget where God picked us from, from the pit or valley God delivered us; we are sometimes too quick to forget. But like Joel Osteen rightly said, we need to pass God's goodness to others so they can pass it to the next generation as well. I listened to one of Joyce Meyer's numerous messages where she said she promised herself to write up to 100 books before she dies so that even when she is gone, the next generation after her can still hear about the wonderful works of God. And she does this by putting into books every stage of her life, how God delivered her and set her free. She wants them to know that there is a God and if He can help and deliver her, He can do likewise for them.

She promised to leave a legacy of God's goodness to her decedents. During the message, she said most of the books God used to minister to her were books written in the 1930s, so she believes the next four generations will be blessed by her books. How true this is! If only most of us believers will have this attitude in life, we will leave a lasting legacy of God that will point our descendants to Him. What are you leaving for your descendants after your life is spent on earth?

The aftermath of the storm is likened to the aftermath of the hurricane. It is followed with clearing of debris and damages caused by the storm because there is usually nothing good that is left. But with God, the aftermath of the storm means the beginning of bright colors like the rainbow which we read in the book of Genesis after the destruction of the earth. God always help his children to start afresh and rebuild after the storm. He restores and replenishes them in all that they have lost and sometimes like in the case of Job, restores more than was lost. The rainbow in Genesis signifies the end of every storm both now and in the future. The bible says in the book of Job that God blessed Job more than what he lost. *Job 42:12 - So the LORD blessed the latter end of Job more than his beginning: for he had fourteen thousand sheep, and six thousand camels, and a thousand yoke of oxen, and a thousand she asses.*

Confession

This is my season of double portion blessings; all I have lost in the storm of life is now released back to me in great measures. I decree, the harvest that God has for me in this season, no Amalekites can stop or destroy it. I am rightly positioned to receive my harvest because now is my due time. My rainbow has been raised in the sky for all to see, so what has already been done by the Lord can no longer be undone by men, evil agents and spiritual forces. My storm of destruction and pain has receded. I am out of the storm of shame, barrenness, bitterness, poverty, sickness, hypocrisy, marital turbulence, business failure, career failure, and childlessness, failure in ministry and whatever that has been a storm in my life is over this day in Jesus Name. Amen!

– Blessing Bassey.

When Noah and his family came out of the storm, they started afresh in a clean land on earth. God is starting afresh with you this season. You might find yourself in a new place doing new things like a new career, relationship, business, ministry, and marriage (that is, rebirthing your marriage or helping you to start again). Whatever level he is starting with you please embrace it and trust him because you are OUT OF THE STORM. Bishop Oyedepo (Winners Chapel) once shared a testimony of a woman in his church that the word of knowledge came to one faithful service that the lord said she should start selling roasted groundnut, she did not look at it as a job or business for people of no class, she obeyed and before months she became an employer of labor, nobody knew what this woman has been going through as a storm in her career or business but on that fateful day she came OUT OF THE STORM. That word you have been waiting for is already released to you.

Sometimes after the storm, we might still be experiencing little storms, like in the case of Noah in Genesis. Even though the storm was over, there was still flood of water on the floor. He and his family had to wait for some more days for the water to recede. The same applies to our lives, sometimes and for some people, after the storm is over, they still experience some little difficulties; bit by bit till the situation completely changes. This is why we need to stand in faith after the storm and keep checking just as Noah did in Genesis 8:7, *And he sent forth a raven, which went forth to and fro, until the waters were dried up from off the earth.* It rained "cats and dogs" for 40 days and 40 nights, enough to flood the entire earth and kill everything that wasn't on Noah's ark. After all that, God remembered his promise to Noah to keep him and all his loved ones safe. So, he sent a wind that ended the storm. God will remember you just as He remembered Noah and his family.

God will always remember His children no matter how long the storm lasts. When the time came for Joseph to come out of the storm of life, the bible said the word of God came and tried him and within 24 hours Joseph clothes were changed, he shaved and came to the King's presence very clean. Joseph's restoration, blessings and harvest was immediate. He rose from being a prisoner to becoming a Prime Minister in one day. This is accelerated promotion. ***Psalm 105:17-20 - He sent a man before them, even Joseph, who was sold for a servant: Whose feet they hurt with fetters: he was laid in iron: Until the time that his word came: the word of the LORD tried him. The king sent and loosed him; even the ruler of the people, and let him go free.***

I don t know if you have been held in physical or spiritual chains like Joseph, the good thing is that everyone that has a say both physically and spiritually to your release will have no choice but to let you go free because the storm is over and you are OUT OF THE STORM. The above bible verse says the king sent and lost him, even the ruler of the people. Every physical and spiritual King that has been ruling over your life will have a change of mind and let you go free just because the storm is over in Jesus name

But in the case of Noah, the bible says Noah was asleep at the time, but the silence woke him up on the day God stopped the rain. He knew something was different, because for so long, it seemed, rain was pouring down, and that was all anyone could hear. Except that day, all he could hear were the waves pounding into the side of the ark.

He ran through the boat and woke everyone else up. "It's finally over!" he exclaimed. "Let's all give thanks to God for stopping the rain and saving us!" Noah got used to the storm that even when God stopped the storm he was still asleep but woke up and shouted the storm is finally over. It is a season to give thanks to God for bringing the storm to an end finally after a long time. Sometimes after the storm we still feel as if we are still in the storm because like Noah we get used to the storm and shaking off the feeling of the storm takes a while. All we need to do at this stage is to give thanks to God, praising and rejoicing before his presence on every opportunity that we have. This might not come easy to most of us but God himself will grant us the grace, because at this stage in life we all seem to be tired. We need to be grateful to God and appreciate him by thanking him for the journey and bringing us out.

Now, even though the storm had stopped, the earth was still covered with water. It took 150 days for the water to recede enough so that everyone could get off onto dry land. He first let the raven off, who flew around until the waters dried up, because they originally were higher than the mountains by about 20 feet. Next he let the dove off, three times. The first time was nothing special, but the second time, the dove carried an olive branch back in its beak. The third time, the dove never returned to the ark.

At first Noah sent a raven that was going to and fro bringing back a situation report till the water dried up completely, and then Noah and his family came out. After the storm there is a tendency for us to want to rush into doing things such as trying to get back on our feet as fast as possible, but it is very important for us to wait to know when God is saying it is okay to go out. At the end of a storm, we need to be patient and wait on God to hear from Him. It is not the time to rush into making decisions or taking actions. The bible said Noah kept checking till it was clear and okay for him and his family to continue their normal life. For many (including very good myself), we rush to make decisions as soon as the storm is over.

Remember Noah and his family gave thanks to God for saving their lives and stopping the storm. When God heard the thanks coming up to heaven from Noah's family, he promised never to destroy all living creatures again. As a sign of this promise from God, he made a rainbow.

Genesis 9:13 -15; I do set my bow in the cloud, and it shall be for a token of a covenant between me and the earth. And it shall come to pass, when I bring a cloud over the earth, that the bow shall be seen in the cloud: And I will remember my covenant, which is between me and you and every living creature of all flesh; and the waters shall no more become a flood to destroy all flesh. God said. "I will never again upset the normal processes of nature," the Lord promised.

Has God ever rescued you or someone you care about from a storm? I am sure he has, and more than once at that. Did you offer God your thanks at those times? How have you responded to God delivering you from the storm in the past? Did you always realize that only God could save you? Don't forget to give him thanks.

After the big celebration comes the big celebration, we are elevated above all that we can ever imagine, we are positioned for great testimony, and we become living testimonies for the world to see that God is the only one that can deliver and restore all that we have lost. This is a season of joy, praise and thanksgiving. It is a season to show gratitude to God for all that he has done and to expect and take that which He is offering to us. The blessing that comes after the storm is that God makes everything new again.

Job made the right choice in the midst of the storm. This is very relevant to us so as to understand how much will be restored back to us at the end of our storm, and how the restoration will come about. Job made the right choice by forgiving his enemies and friends for all they did to him during the storm, and just for this single act, God restored more than what he had lost and blessed him.

I am confident that when we make the right choices in any storm, we can reap immense blessings.

Job 42:10 - The LORD restored the fortunes of Job when he prayed for his friends, and the LORD increased all that Job had twofold. King James Bible (Cambridge Ed.)

During the storm people are definitely going to insult you and say all manner of things concerning you, but immediately after the storm you have to forgive them and move on. It is written that we should forgive others their trespasses so that our heaven father will also forgive us.

Matthew 6:15 - But if ye forgive not men their trespasses, neither will your Father forgive your trespasses.

A TESTIMONY BY ALISON LAICHTER

After the storm, I felt a collective rush of gratitude and a deep empathy for those in need. It was like being sick and then feeling thankful for returned health. It reminded me of when I first learned to pay attention to the simple act of breathing. What a miracle, I remember thinking, that even when I breathe all of the air out, it returns faithfully, all on its own. What a blessing, to feel, in your own breath, the work of creation – culled from: ***Breathing and Blessings After the Storm by Alison Laichter, Executive Director, The Jewish Meditation Center***

I don't know what you might have gone through as a storm but the good news is that it is your time to be blessed and favored by God. God is saying to you now; your storm is over, it is enough, it is your season to shine and radiate the glory of God. The veil covering your glory has just been removed by the lord. The bible says when Jesus Christ gave up the ghost on the cross of Calvary the veil covering the temple was torn into two. Where it has be the priest only going into the temple or holy of holiest, after the storm, when the veil was torn into two, the temple was revealed and everyone who accepted Jesus now had access to the holy of holies; there was made possible an easy passage to see the lord as every intermediary was removed. Whatever has been a storm over your life, marriage, immigration, family, children, business, ministry or whatever it is that has been troubling you has given way today. You can now access your destiny walking through those open doors that the devil or household enemies shut hitherto.

Matthew 27:51- Jesus, when he had cried again with a loud voice, yielded up the ghost. And, behold, the veil of the temple was rent in twain from the top to the bottom; and the earth did quake, and the rocks rent; And the graves were opened; and many bodies of the saints which slept arose,

The bible said when Jesus rose up from the grave; he led captivity captive and gave gifts unto men. As you rise up from the storm which has been a grave to you, I see you receiving your gifts from Jesus to manifest your destiny and potential. In the book of Judges 6, when the storm of idol worshipping came to an end in Gideon's life and village, Gideon who was very weak in strength and character became a mighty man of valor. Apparently, he was a simple man living a very ordinary life. I don't know what area of your life people have seen and considered weak; my beloved, your real identity and personality is not known by any man but God, and it is about to be announced to the world because your storm is over. When Mary and Mary Magdalene got to the tomb of Jesus, they found the tomb empty and the angel of God they met there asked them if it was Jesus of Nazareth they were looking for. They said yes, and he said to them, "He is longer here, He has risen", oh! My beloved, people will look for you where they left you before or expect to find you there, but do you know what, they will hear a heavenly broadcaster telling them that you are on your way to Galilee, to the upper room; you place of promotion and destiny, and there will be an announcement concerning your change of location. Remember the angel they met at the tomb of Jesus said "He is gone ahead of you to Galilee, there you will find Him". EVERYONE LOOKING FOR YOU WILL FIND YOU AT THE TOP. YOU ARE OUT OF THE STORM!

Mathew 28 - After the Sabbath, at dawn on the first day of the week, Mary Magdalene and the other Mary went to look at the tomb.

2 There was a violent earthquake, for an angel of the Lord came down from heaven and, going to the tomb, rolled back the stone and sat on it. 3 His appearance was like lightning,

and his clothes were white as snow. 4 The guards were so afraid of him that they shook and became like dead men.

5 The angel said to the women, "Do not be afraid, for I know that you are looking for Jesus, who was crucified. 6 He is not here; he has risen, just as he said. Come and see the place where he lay. 7 Then go quickly and tell his disciples: 'He has risen from the dead and is going ahead of you into Galilee. There you will see him.' Now I have told you."

8 So the women hurried away from the tomb, afraid yet filled with joy, and ran to tell his disciples. 9 Suddenly Jesus met them. "Greetings," he said. They came to him, clasped his feet and worshiped him. 10 Then Jesus said to them, "Do not be afraid. Go and tell my brothers to go to Galilee; there they will see me."

Jesus was buried naked but my beloved, he rose up fully dressed in a rich raiment. You will change awesomely in appearance and personality at the end of your storm that people, even your close relatives will not be able to recognize you let alone your enemies. In Genesis when Joseph came in contact with his brothers, they could not recognize him because they never expected him to be at such a prestigious position and a place of class, authority, affluence, abundance, riches and so much wealth. Those that sold you into the storm you went through only hasten your destiny and propelled you into your blessing through the storm. I am hearing you say you will forgive them so God can showcase you like my brother in law, Jesus Christ (who forgave his enemies while still on the cross), and Joseph who already forgave his brothers who sold him into slavery even before they showed up in Egypt. Just like Esau too who God gave back his lost blessing and birthright?

Like Jesus Christ, sometimes, you are already out of the storm spiritually but physically your release and freedom seems not to be manifesting for all to see, like I could see through the tomb that Jesus Christ might have risen but was trapped inside it; He must have been saying to His heavenly father, it is time for me to come out physically, I can't keep sitting here inside the tomb remember, the bible said in Matthew 28:2, that there was an earthquake and the angel of the lord from heaven came and roll away the stone blocking the door to the tomb. Every stone that is still blocking your final release from the storm or whatever it is that is holding your total release from the storm is receiving a divine visitation today and will definitely give way for you to exit to your abundance and manifestation of the glory of God just because YOU ARE OUT OF THE STORM. Whether you are still inside the tomb or outside, just keep praising God because the truth is that you are out of the storm.

I want you to know that people will doubt your release from the storm, and as a result will still want to ridicule you, even despite and in spite of the evidence they are seeing but stand your ground and maintain your joy and celebrate your victory.

Mathew 28:16-20 - Then the eleven disciples went to Galilee, to the mountain where Jesus had told them to go. 17 When they saw him, they worshiped him; but some doubted. 18 Then Jesus came to them and said, "All authority in heaven and on earth has been given to me. 19 Therefore go and make disciples of all nations, baptizing them in the name of the Father and of the Son and of the Holy Spirit, 20 and teaching them to obey everything I have commanded you. And surely I am with you always, to the very end of the age."

Despite that some of the people and disciples doubted if it was Jesus, he still went ahead to complete his assignment by ordaining the disciples for the great commission.

Sometimes ago back in Nigeria, there was a time I used to be scared of going home after work because of fear. Whenever I close my eyes to sleep at night, I imagine there is a snake in my room and I will not be able to sleep, so I will end up sleeping at the church and going to work from there as I usually go with change of clothes for the next day. This continued for a while until one day when I got to the church for a prayer vigil, I found the door shut and locked because the vigil was cancelled and I was not informed, and since I couldn't enter the church, I had no other choice than to go back home, on my way home I said to myself, "whatever serpent is waiting to kill me tonight, let them come that tonight it's either they kill me or sometime will happen. Beloved, do you know as soon as my head hit the pillow I slept off and didn't wake up until the next morning, and that night was the best night I had a good sleep in weeks. What am I saying here? THE STORM WAS ALREADY OVER AND I WAS OUT OF IT DIDN'T REALIZE IT TILL THERE WAS NOWHERE TO HIDE ANYMORE. This was the incident God used to destroy the yoke of fear of going to bed or staying alone at home. When you know the power in the blood of Jesus and the God you serve, you will speak to whatever it is that is trying to stand between you and your victory. I believe Jesus spoke to the door of the tomb to open which urgently caused the angel from heaven to show up and roll away the store.

Psalm 24:7-10 - Lift up your heads, O ye gates; and be ye lift up, ye everlasting doors; and the King of glory shall come in.

8 Who is this King of glory? The Lord strong and mighty, the Lord mighty in battle.

9 Lift up your heads, O ye gates; even lift them up, ye everlasting doors; and the King of glory shall come in.

10 Who is this King of glory? The Lord of hosts, he is the King of glory.

The above bible passage can be used to violently command you stepping out of your hiding place after the storm.

REJOICE! For the storm is over and you are out of the storm. There is a miracle coming your way. Be expectant because it is a new season and receive your miracle.

When Prophet Elijah was praying for the rain to fall, he asked his servant, Gehazi to keep checking for a sign, until Gehazi came back and said he saw a sign like the hand of a man, and Prophet Elijah said that is it! From a little hand came a mighty downpour. What are we saying here? We pray without checking for a sign at all or we check but not persistently. Remember, Prophet Elijah asked his servant to keep checking until the 7th time before he saw a sign. Why did Prophet Elijah show this desperate attitude? The answer is that he knew that once he pray, God will surely answer him.

41 And Elijah said unto Ahab, Get thee up, eat and drink; for there is a sound of abundance of rain.

42 So Ahab went up to eat and to drink. And Elijah went up to the top of Carmel; and he cast himself down upon the earth, and put his face between his knees,

43 Kings 18: 43- 46, And said to his servant, Go up now, look toward the sea. And he went up, and looked, and said, there is nothing. And he said, Go again seven times.

44 And it came to pass at the seventh time, that he said, Behold, there ariseth a little cloud out of the sea, like a man's hand. And he said, Go up, say unto Ahab, Prepare thy chariot, and get thee down that the rain stops thee not.

45 And it came to pass in the meanwhile, that the heaven was black with clouds and wind, and there was a great rain. And Ahab rode, and went to Jezreel.

46 And the hand of the Lord was on Elijah; and he girded up his loins, and ran before Ahab to the entrance of Jezebel.

A new job, a new career, a new home, a new marriage, a new relationship, a new health devoid of diseases, a new business, a new anointing.

How you handle this stage of your life will determine your level of promotion. In the name of Jesus Christ I command you to receive grace and a new anointing to pray till you not only hear the sound of rain but see, feel and use it. Even before Prophet Elijah prayed he told King Ahab, "Go up, eat and drink; for there is the sound of abundance of rain." It is a time to enjoy the abundance of God.

When you find the river that God is flowing, jump in and flow with it. – Pastor Benny Hinn.

CONCLUSION:

PRAYER FOR REMOVING HINDRANCES TO ADVANCEMENT AND DEMOLISHING STUMBLING BLOCKS

Thank the lord because He alone can advance you.

O Lord, bring me into favor with all those who will decide on my advancement.

I reject the spirit of the tail and I claim the spirit of the head, in the name of Jesus.

O Lord, transfer, remove or change all human agents that are bent on stopping my advancement.

I receive the anointing to excel above my contemporaries in the name of Jesus.

O Lord, catapult me into greatness as You did Daniel in the land of Babylon.

O lord, help me to identify and deal with any weakness in me that can hinder my greatness.

O Lord, dispatch your angels to roll away every stumbling block to my promotion, advancement and elevation.

O, Lord restore all my wasted years and efforts and covert them to blessings, in the name of Jesus.

I lose angels to go and create favor in my finances, career, business, marriage and other areas of my life.

O Lord, like Joseph brings me into favor with all those that will decide my case.

Let all my blessings held captive locally or overseas be released to me in the name of Jesus.

Let men bless me everywhere I go.

Father, by yours favor, accelerate my journey to success.

Father by your favor, make a way for me in the wilderness of life.

NOTE

Some of the declarations were extracted from: Commanding Your Morning by Cindy Trimm.

Bibliography

Rev. Fr. George, C. Matthew: Suffering - Overcoming The Storms of Life

Printed in the USA
CPSIA information can be obtained
at www.ICGtesting.com
LVHW051147131023
760674LV00050B/785